The Plum-Stone Game

Ahsahta Press

The New Series

Number 26

The Plum-Stone Game

Kathleen Jesme

Boise State University • Boise • Idaho • 2009

Ahsahta Press, Boise State University
Boise, Idaho 83725
http://ahsahtapress.boisestate.edu
http://ahsahtapress.boisestate.edu/books/jesme/jesme.htm

Printed in the United States of America
Cover art: "One and a half sisters" © 2003 by Maggie Taylor.
Cover design by Quemadura
Book design by Janet Holmes
First printing January 2009
ISBN-13: 978-1-934103-03-6

Library of Congress Cataloging-in-Publication Data

Jesme, Kathleen, 1949-
The plum-stone game / Kathleen Jesme.
    p. cm. -- (The new series ; no. 26)
ISBN 978-1-934103-03-6 (pbk. : alk. paper)
I. Title.

PS3610.E86P56 2008
811'.6—DC22

                                    2008009078

ACKNOWLEDGMENTS

Thanks to the following publications in which these poems first appeared: *Babel Fruit*, "I will not let thee go except thou bless me," (I-VII); *Coconut*, "Lives of the Saints"; *Conduit* [from "Curation" (fig. i, fig. ii, fig. iii, fig. vi, fig. x, fig. xiv)]; *Prairie Schooner* (from "The Little Hour": "Whistle," "Homage," "My old dog"); and *Tiferet* ["It looks like rain"; from "The Little Hour": "What is green in me," "The mantel clock," "View from the upstairs window" (I and III)].

Contents

Lives of the Saints

I began as a darkness and remained so. My life was lit by occasional flares toward which I groped unevenly. I had no mother and no father to speak of. Then you came and it was a big midnight into which the empty stars had been sucked. All that was left were the curved streaks of their paths sliding through space as we turned on our axis and turned around our sun, and turned around our galaxy and turned once more. There was no turning point. All was darkness.

I was a schemer. I lit lamps in unlikely places to attract night's insects. I knew nothing of the day. Words sunk in me like ships crushed in an ice floe. I nursed hiddenness. Took on meaning. Imbibed the sound of thunder. I waited for things to come by and trapped them. My father told me that wild things will not suffer containment. I learned by entrapment. I learned by the sound of my knees sliding through fall leaves. I entered and left by the smallest of holes, like a bat. I peeked when I was supposed to cover my eyes. I saw things I was not intended to see. I told. I didn't tell. I said. I didn't say. I hid in the least spaces.

I was most ordinary and began as a thing. You didn't know me. We missed each other by minutes—I made up words to explain it. At 12 I found something that was like you but was not you. I began to follow it. It led me everywhere. I fed it from a saucer on the chipped linoleum. I kept it lit.

I was a great liar and told many tales that were true. I had suitcases ready at all times. I followed anacondas and slipstreams. Sometimes I took them down. I tried to remake the noise. I sat for examination. I was full of puncture holes. Marks appeared on my body overnight, as if from dreaming. I climbed the ladder from Hell and crossed. My robe trailed behind me and caught in the slats because already I was not tall enough for it.

I was a boy like other boys, except that I had murdered my sister. There was a lot of atonement required. I made up a past and a future. I visited wombs and their prisoners. I brought music whenever I could. The credo was one I decided to live by. They called me another name than the one I was born with. Then my name broke and had to be replaced. I was one of the chosen; I rejoiced in the lamb. I went this way instead of that.

I was a product of despair. There was a river of dying, and I floated in on it. Others were leaving, and I was coming. There is no cure for that. I found pinpricks of light that absorbed me. I wanted to keep looking. I was through before I even began: I could see the finishing point right from the start. I could hear moles burrow and squeak underground; I thought I must be an owl, but I was not. I learned to dissemble.

Once, finding a hole in the ground, I passed over it. I was taught to call it God. My life has been the same ever since. It could not have been I who did that. I am more like a field than anything, although receptiveness liquefies me. I had a childhood once, and wanted to keep it. Everything else has been lost in the general conflagration.

Although I had parents and a family, I was approached by other orphans. I took what I could from them. I tried to build with stones. I emptied the expanses of my body. I found the other thing and tried to hide it but it beat me every morning with a stick until I submitted. I found that staring at the ceiling created a conversation I liked. I knew it was not-me, but I couldn't believe it. I honored the muffled sounds of fucking that came through the wall. I kept a crow call in my dresser drawer for future needs.

I couldn't stand my insides. The stinking of blood and the fush of organs working. I stood along the railroad track wanting to crawl under the train. The star inside me grew larger. It began to show through a mark growing on my leg and the white scars on my fingers from pocketknives. I learned how to penetrate numbers. I crossed the portal of time gleefully. I grew a row of nipples on my chest. That is how I became who I am.

I learned one thing and learned it well. I photosynthesized sunlight and procreated by scattering seedlings. I tried the patience of the gods, you and she. I copied others. I came to the end quicker than expected. I died on a bed of apples. I wanted to come back as a mother's ghost. I wanted to see my tears, but it was late, and the lights had gone out all over the city. I opened my eyes without asking and saw them blink back on. One by one.

The Little Hour

Whistle

She is like an animal, all desire—without language
to staunch it

but she can tell that her kind are different: something when they move
their mouths

tremor she can't imitate
   can't get their attention

even the shadow of sound—

Grass sweet and smooth after mowing
ammonia-sharp in the hot sun
soft and prickly—

I pick a blade and whistle

she puts her fingers to the reed
opens her mouth and feels my throat:

nothing but my imagination reaches beyond the limits of her body

The lovely darkness behind you

    the doorway

    your frame: some of what spills
    from the body seems to have
    its own light

    or when it falls, takes
    immediately what light there is

    from the air—

    we had photographs to confine
    the light; nothing
    to recall

    sound

The mantel clock

ticks quietly just inside hearing
a little hitch in the beat and the house makes its rounds
under-water

the dogs' breathing
waves
that lap the shore

beneath another line of sound
only when the wind stops
but it never does

something like crickets another time of year a far-off field at twilight

something like a voice
a day inside

open and break
upon us

Small sphere

                my tiny planet
        among giants
        orb of my body

        turning—oh not true
        that space
        holds no sound: here

        your voice around me
        the dust of stars
        spinning into being and then

        that other hour: dark
        lustrous
        and endless

        endless
        and lustrous
        that other hour: dark

        spinning into being and then
        the dust of stars
        your voice around me

        holds no sound: here
        that space
        turning—oh not true

        orb of my body
        among giants
        small sphere my tiny planet

Homage

All I am acquainted with, absolute solitary. Arrival:
pinpricks of stars. *Alpha Centauri*. Alien. *Asellus Secundus*.
Until my glasses came. After that counting: avert face.

Bent backs lean together whispering. Sound
carries bees. Automatic breath. *Betelgeuse*.
A blueprint for old idioms.

Coracle of the divine child. *Chara*. Carrion boat.
My glasses come. Closer than we knew. Pick up
and carry/crown our vastness. Circumference.

Double stars aplenty. *Diadem* of stars. Stars smoky
in the dust sky: a warm-day-in-early-spring smoky.
Path of dirt. Decant.

Eyes so compressed the scant body falters. To arrange
the central fjord, a frame of mind. *Fum al Samakah*.
Entrance the foreign. Flanks of the sullen creature.

Gianfar. Glissade and glissando. Steps into the giddy:
when all the stars came down for us. *Gorgonea Secunda*.
Glasses gaunt.

Haunt me with your heaven; hover me;
cover me. *Head of Hydrus*. Her hands held up. Theories of
inversion. *Izar*. Intimate meaning.

Jabber. *Jabbah*. Ordinary journey through dark-
hearted country. Worry the kith and kin to my adoption.
Kaus Borealis. Kangaroo mother awaiting young.

Linked to a twisted swallow. The shape of linger, leaven
of organs. *Lupus*. Lingua franca: devices of the soul. Leave me
in the loud grass to pry.

Messier objects: midsummer, and the crickets rub their legs
and sigh. Meteorites secure atmosphere. Mother me. Nonsense;
necessary failure. Not this–not that. *Owl Nebula*.

Oil slicking down skin. No oral memory. You grant one dark
and thin wish. *Orion*. History of one who dropped
the orb into my outstretched palm.

Praesepe, the Beehive Cluster. Pneuma. Places we haven't assumed.
Putting my feet into the fire. *Quasar*. The quarter hour:
quarter notes risen through the feet.

Reception-transmission-expression. *Rigel Kentaurus*. Rolling
land, high grass reaching my chin. Raising hope. Release
of the strange noise, heart bleating from the inside.

Show me your stars. Show you mine. Shout and heed.
See how the body wants. Scant harvest. Stroked coat
of the good dog. Sharp spruce needles driving my fingers along.

Tree out of ground, I grew slowly. Entertained trajectory. Teacher.
Terebellum. Until my glasses came. Interrupting. Undoing.
Uncover the body's tender ledges. *Ursas* great and small.

Vibration. Variations. My voice the loneliest sound
you ever heard. *Vulpecula.* To have made something divine.
How I visualize your face: with hills.

Wild duck cluster. Way out of the world without word.
What green is: I think I know. A smell, a sharp while ago.
Wires that mock space and outrun time.

X-ray stars. What we give each. The lives we might have had.
If I don't know you. *Yildun.* Yield. Yes to the sudden break, yes
to the thunder. *Zosma. Zibal.* Zero made of nothing.

In June or July

Rain with no wind: bells of water hang on the trees
each holds the entire sky

Green becomes oppressive at some point
in June or July

as everything does

She uses the smallest sensual experience—
her fingers pulling apart the tiny rootlets of peat moss
and then separating the plants—they don't want
to be separated

they don't want to stand alone
in a field of dark dirt planted against the sun

don't want that kind of distinctness
would prefer to stay commingled
small social unproductive

but planting continues and there is a harvest
to look for
plenty of rain

Matter attracts matter

1.

Have ever wanted to swim in a lightning storm
My father calls me out of the water

I would send you the worm of myself
If I thought you would open me

Dereliction taken for granted on a ruby day
Shining in all its commonplace

The earth reaches for the apple of light
The extent to which I reach depends on you

Not with the scarcity, but with the fullness
Not with the match, but with the flame

The light comes down around us
Strokes the nave of our bodies

I catch you, fish, barehanded
You must have wanted to come to me

The plow blade strokes the snow
A scythe in the winter field

2.

The plow blade strokes the snow
Strokes the nave of our bodies

You must have wanted to come to me
Not with scarcity, but with fullness

My father calls me out of the water
Shining in all its commonplace

I thought you would open me
Dereliction taken for granted on a ruby day

Have ever wanted to swim in a lightning storm
The earth reaches for the apple of light

The extent to which I reach depends on you
A scythe in the winter field

I would send you the worm of myself
Not with the match, but with the flame

I catch you, fish, barehanded
The light comes down around us

View from the upstairs window

After a day of high wind
wings banging at the window a blur of dark
the screen vibrating
an open space:
larger than it was before
drawing the eye out into October and its strings of light

Leaves shifting from yesterday's angry mobs
depleted now
quiet:
so I began to see the bird long after
its wings stopped beating at the pane:
I started to say leaves
but stopped when the wings

carried my eye out into the garden

View from the upstairs window

A long wall of broken stones

a broken wall stretching out past what can be seen

a wall with breaks in the stones

an unbroken line: grandmother carrying water

to the cemetery

in two equally weighted buckets

My old dog feels her way with her tongue

to where the water is
in the bucket—can no longer see it:

water is hard to see
even with clear eyes

I thread the needle with my tongue
my good eye

He gave her his pocket watch

because she had found the pulsing chain

and questioned it with her fingers:
He let her feel her way to that small treasure

she had no expectations
and everything was bright

so brilliant in the moment of cognition
nothing obscured the self—

we need to see and hear
ourselves to camouflage—

and he thought
how easy it would be to use her

Perfectionism requires a great deal of cruelty

and she is cruel
and I am the bell she rings
and rings

Give me yourself
Give me your
self
and I will make such music of it

I can feel my tongue
clapping against the sides

and the deep dong dong
of my helpless love

View from the upstairs window

I saw something from the corner of my eye,
working and yet unfocused, for a moment,
by the sudden disappearance of what I didn't know
until that moment existed. I ran down the stairs

to the back door, out into the empty field,
already harvested, nothing but grain stubble.
The pheasants startled up, their wings clapping
a warning. And a door closed. A door.

Bone ends: radius ulna fibula

carpa and tarsa

parts of the body that ambulate
hold and feed
and grasp

all laid across
by light in the west: afternoon disembarks

marks bodies

she can feel them as well as anyone: she knows
by hand

but with knowing comes
a turn aslant
sense of being skirted
separation unlike anything—

more the *spirit* of separation—

she wants to go down to the body
root in it and its inhabitants

she will not be turned aside

Yes I said turn off the light

     it changes everything

     —if she'd been unable to scream

     but she found her voice

"What is green in me"

lightens
and falls away gold

scattering
strikes the wind

I dreamed of catching two dark fish
on one hook:
one had only a head

cast deep and address the wind:

when one thing
disappears

the hidden
shows

I am alone here: let me move

Let me dig
in a place where there are
others

Let me lift
the others out and hand them
over

Rise and fall

There's not a place here that I don't remember
nothing I can't recall about you—

I had a child once
and she grew too big for me

I had a child once
and the world took her

Curation

FIG. I

Lave biface with denticulate edge
Sidestruck flake, lava from a waterworn boulder
No tools—the difficulty of digging
Cast with copper loopshank
Not yet opened
150. E. Cloverleaf, M-3 east
A woman's game, five plum stones
Then, after we had gone back to look

FIG. 2

Single carved bird head facing outward
Pouch contains quills
Used in Plum-Stone game, time in suspension
Trying to sense the body
88" (Simms Number) bumps under the big gashes on the side
Enter the gaps between, nothing else wanting
When 2 moons and 3 black or 2 stars and 3 black or 2 moons and 3
    white turn up it is called 'Hu-be' (mysterious)
Tetrameter bird—Jickadeedeedee
We can no longer return to it

~

Curatorial Comment: Goes with (b–f) painted plum seed dice
(d) and (f) have a crescent moon on one side and star on other
(b) (c) (e) all black on one side and natural on other
(g) stick counters made from blue joint grass
Stones found, nothing on the ground

FIG. 3

Broken-restored Bird bowl pierced for holes
What stops only at having, wet from all the rain
Ararat Sector, 1 mile above Siloa
Measure of our capacity
Fragment remains come and go again
What we might have seen there
Washed out complete—one of them breaks open
Probable infant burial
They want the sky

FIG. 4

Fragments of Catlow Twine basketry, warps and other plied parts
Overwhemingly Z-twisted and made of two s-spun elements
May have thrown out, or false embroidery
Were all of relatively late date
No lessons from memory
Before they realize the child is gone—wished away—
Or twined counter-clockwise
Radiocarbon dated to 4430+/− 60 years ago
Across small space she had to see herself
Arriving later than the animal body
Navigate with another sense
Not to give her time to fill with terror
Represent intrusions from elsewhere in the Basin rather than *in situ*
    developments
Measure of reach: waiting for time to come and take her away

FIG. 5

Redware fired pottery jar, edge of her appearance
Pinched in at waist forming two bulges in body
Finding things she should not—
Or whatever is at the rim—
Yellow glaze streaked with dark manganese splotches
Sky cobalt just before sunrise
Then she passed by making glancing contact
And the child inside
And the one inside that

FIG. 6

Incised figure of a bird, mostly goes unnoticed
Exterior unglazed except for light splashes
She had nothing we would try to take
But captured instead
As if waiting for us to arrive
Cobalt blue on the body where the handles are attached
As two persons
The blue dark contrast with the body tones
Completely invisible—
Interior is Albany slip

FIG. 7

Wooden container with hinged domed cover
Adjustments made all night long, they take and take
All corners mitered, painted black with swag and spray
The work of the same hand
Appears on
Front lock plate in place but hasp missing
Interior lined with a plain paper, no handle on cover
But eventually drops down
Slips away

FIG. 8

Large unfinished ash burl bowl, desiccated condition
Into the sight line, if not for her hunger
Exterior retains shape and rough texture of original surface
Carried a long time, undercut, quantity poured out
Those that are left
Small thieves of her sorrow slipping in
Some axe marks where burl was separated from tree
To undergo one form of disintegration or fire
Interior cavity roughly formed with axe but not finished
Enough to weaken, shows deep axe cuts
Never used as a bowl

FIG. 9 [MISSING]

Well-made hand-carved bowl of nearly circular shape
Pouring spout, thin-walled and lightweight
Can be assumed to have had a constant rate through time
Handed down intact, with what remains
Outside edge of rim is chamfered, may have been turned on a lathe
Inside and out, the hand
No evidence of chopping but interior bottom is darkened and eroded as
    if some caustic material had been kept in it
No picture available

Burial urn with particularly ornate white, black, yellow, and red slip
   paint scheme compared to the other three urns
No heat from inside the body
Painted with a pattern of black spots resembling fur coat of jaguar
Spots still distinct after a thousand years of burial
Restless earth, likeness carried for a long while
Equality made possible by capture
A jaguar-human figure perches on the lid

FIG. II

Symmetrical and very deep, the deep cleaves
More of them here, we wait
Thick sides and bottom smooth finish
The time it takes to adapt to the light passing through the interior
Deeply scarred from use as a chopping bowl
Color change inside suggests water or other liquid left to stand
Possibly used as a milk pan

FIG. 12

Had not yet opened, no memory again
One castellation has carved cutout handle
The other is solid with three finger notches carved with a small gouge
    or a crooked knife
Heavy and thick-walled, fence for her small thefts
The unprotected part—rather crudely finished, axe marks clearly evident
Exterior eruptive red, interior extensively scarred
Offer not taken

FIG. 13

Barrel-shaped jug with nipples
Nothing enters yet nothing stays inside
Concentric profusion of circle motifs wrapped about the body
Her brightest costume had not been touched by anyone
A ladder motif in the body-neck join
Busy doing little works, pity her limbs
Ground red and yellow splattered
Dark disappearing with rain

FIG. 14

Mended from fragments with later additions
We found things easily removed but not accurately replaced
No more than two-thirds of its capacity
Opposed to the breach, flat everted rim uneven in places
A slight bending toward us, yet pronounced
Loose and running under
Surface wear and breakage on the body have destroyed some features
Applied over slip, summer-dark again
With all its unfinished things, the day can't reverse them
Back slightly curved and plain with circular firing-hole
One holding each breast, multiple amulets cascade from the neck
Night work shed little light
Flows through the difficult handles of speech

FIG. 15

Deep carinated body, day of four nights
Each form of mourning reclaims her
Memory stands closer to the moon
High splayed foot with rim slightly everted
Under a layer lighter shade of same on the inside
Point at which there can be a relic, found
Incised decoration embellished in green
Tangential near-circular motifs around rim
Or as is often the case—
Remains itself and the opposite of itself
In tondo frontal device: woman in a knee-length robe flanked by shiny
    rods in twining serpentine lines

It looks like

It looks like

    rain
               all round me now. No verbs.
Nothing so sparrow as that.

The blue tarpaulin, unfolded square, stretches
over baled straw, remedy for a gray sky.
I am the window. Not the door. She
            is the wind not the sand.

Before rain: inside is contained
not as in open air:
            ozone slots through the gaps.

Most of what we call green, figment of another summer,
is actually yellow—possible to see the sun after all
            recombinant with leaves.

    ~

She takes all this and makes a house for it—
honeycombs it, take the sweets
away
leaving the entry sparse and the rooms empty

lets it all drop down
through
a sieve.

    ~

Hail from the storm which still hasn't reached me:
train whirring along the track toward the south.
Words follow each other
            obedient ants in a trail—I heard there's one
                    that stretches hundreds of miles.
I used to stir up ant hills for a thrill as a child—
now I don't need to go looking
for shame.

~

Therefore the expulsion from the garden
the chant of small birds
            the javelin of larger ones
            the mend before the tear
Therefore the plot at one end and the plot at the other
            the dusty smell of old dirt
Therefore sparse time, unreeling and reeling back

~

The scent of lilacs rises to the top
of the house like warm air: I walk up the stairs
            thinking of some woman

                    I wanted to know from childhood—

~

Close attentiveness to the window and what
        is on both sides, as well as
what is on neither.

When she finds the rhythm that corresponds to her skin:
galvanized.

These pockets between feelings: deserts
        between oases. No,
oases between deserts. No

again.

Are we going to work outside?

In the heat.

~

Or yellow and green—
Look how
suddenly it can shift from one
to the other. Notice
that even when we
are sitting side by side looking
at exactly the same thing, our experience is completely
different. Stay awake.

~

Instead, the body

instead of anything else

something solid, steady, sublime

the screeching of young birds demanding to be fed:
the middle of June
the griddle of July

spreading the straw—

~

Yesterday the wind and light made

the young cottonwoods across the road

shimmer like water.

~

This thick rope
coiled, not tied to anything
hanging from a hook
on the shed wall:

I stroke its ropiness
dream its length and suppleness

the lack of form
the way it can only
hang loose
from the hook.

~

Wind sweeps the trees clean
        knocks dead twigs and branches down:

                on the ground they become sticks.

Things fall out of trees—
robin eggs, still blue and full of sky
but empty.

The trees, though, shorn of dead wood,
gesticulate in the wind, pliant,
malleable and so green:

Why don't we have names
                for all the colors of green?

~

The bale splits
open
doesn't much want to fall apart

                    comes away in squares
that we shake out over the mud
raked into
a semblance
of flatness.

There is some straw, but most is what she's weaving into gold: if you squint
a little,
it's gold already.

I will not let thee go except thou bless me

Speak to me fidelities: a shift of traitors each its own
rhyme, each a secret kept discreet. One for the
spackles of light the leaves change, one for the sheets
of fragments. But while she was away, monstrous
hounds grew from her thoughts, tracking. She missed
the feeding. Is it a garden if she didn't interfere is it a
garden if it cannot be left? Now she sees people
canting and wants to turn, awry.

In another country the grasses know her. Are
addressing someone, undressing. 4 inches of rain
times 12 days equals 2: marriages divisible by invisible.
Now she sees people leaving and wants—now that
her father is dead, doesn't seem to care much for
fishing any more. Doesn't tolerate the sight. Not-me.
Not-me. Not for what it can multiply, but for what it
can be broken into. Away the waves. The sheen.

In winter they bisect but now the trees fragment the
—. If she plants grass to cover a scar, would you call
that a garden? Anything that catches light will try to
hold it. Anything that catches sound will give it up.
Wherever the tongue touches. Feeding. A twist of
ground. The inside of a thigh. Furrows you plow.
Twinned seeds: two wings if disconnected. Dizzy
whirling. Intersection of snow and snow.

Shall we examine betrayal? The small lesions on
the skin that begin as ordinary. Try casting them off
into the wind. It grows its yellow seeds, scales of fish,
feathers and fly wings. Pinch them. Today's business
is obedience. She couldn't see anything but green
from the window and the green made her wild.
Make an application to submission. *Who would write
the music?*

She said it is almost necessary to get inside the body
to find its desire. What did she mean, *almost*? Why is
no one crying out in protest? The gaps oh the gaps
they are so large and no one. The mouth hounds its
longing. Wanted to shake the plane of the day flat.
Wanted to cut down anything that rose. She said,
"Everything was ordinary. Not fucking quite."
Things soak up. Out-in, Out-in.

I am not the only one in this haze. Quote. Things
are tuning dark. Eros of error! Blacken in the dusk.
It is our nature to prize. To love. To fill. Our
hands, out like cobwebs, trap whatever falls. How
much further they stretch along a black string.
Singing. Officially, a year of plenty. Someone tunes
the piano: *Jesu, Joy of Man's Desiring*. It's midnight.

Two you. Not me. Equinoxes plow light before us.
Of early summer construe the time: Fifteen hours
eighteen minutes. The fingertip feeling for the
callus along the thumb. The words drop their
feeling on me. Yes you can take. Yesterday had a
hole in it time leaked out. All that white, little
sprinkling of dark. A longing to split the metaphor.

To make the lover of potatoes go away, one must
absent the potatoes from the field. Whatever place
still is. For all our fine intentions. Stirred soup, shirred
cloth. Creeping closer. Don't tell me about meaning
lessness and how language can be used to create it.
Her body, through a thin shirt. Electricity hits the oak
and frees the young trees to spring out. I can almost
read the lighter ones.

Food violates the body, as does love. Pine tar
condenses on the tip of the brush. Pile. Another page.
Gaps in the green. She writes in. There—see the
laundry dangling on that thin wire of wind? How the
spoon fits. People are always asking. Leading to
everything about relationship. Am I allowed to abuse
a word like that? Some days complete themselves;
others wait blankly to be finished.

Insular dense not-available bluebell. Plant of the genus *Endymion*. What does the moon love? *The moon loves those.* A kind of scurrying through words. And so the dusty awkward nameless streets. With out punctuation smooth and seamless and yet and yet. A hoard. A treasure trove. A grove of tall. A board. A mill. The sawn feet. And yet and yet.

Is it a garden if it? For that matter, tell me such unapproachable loveliness. Nevertheless, I am going back. Because to push against is to make firm. And those children curled in the grain of wood on the bedroom door. In the deep pocket of time, we will persist in desire. As if the dark allowed me and the light made me forget. Waits patiently accumulating. To uncover everything. And it almost did.

We have no shells. No bucket to let down. The gap
between the teeth the tongue examines the gap
examined by the tongue. Light banging the screen
behind you can't quite see. Only the wrens bellowing.
Can you hear them? Like seahorses. If sound could
touch you like touch. For longer than I can remember.
Come into view. Facing another way it comes slowly.
Until I find a vein.

Cast. No—look behind. Cast. A blistering day. The
curtains half-shut. A slice of green a grain of yellow a
pinch of blue. Nothing comes by. Four piles of
cinderblocks. How to live in such a yellow season?
It's hard to make a line stretch long when there's
nothing to hold it together. No the blood. No
the river. I said to the dog, *What are we going to do
with you?* Confronted by her overwhelming suffering.

Nothing. Drain it like a pond. Let me take things off: I will go naked among the stones of your love. I will crawl on my knees into the dark field of your affection. Except my own looking. That didn't want to turn. Similarly cut away by *when*. And before it comes again. As when the first absence presents it self and the mind clings to it. Hands that condense the body.

Foreclosure. As when we were forced to decide. As when the dog's condition clearly showed itself. As when we quarreled about nothing. Prose. One inside no math. I admire the silvery backs of the leaves, like new babies' hands. Except my own need to keep nothing but faith. Baffled fate. Keep her from running. Lines narrow and sharp-edged. Satisfaction. Fractions. Stein had a wife/had a life.

Then year. Was year. Each had a long string was like. That hadn't been hadn't been lived hadn't arrived. Parents who never did anything with each other: cut and paste their pictures together. His fingers in her cunt. Imagine it. He is flying an airplane away. She playing the piano and smoking. No. Gave it up for lent. Always on the last page of the past. There is no description for it.

And the ground grew cool and hard and I got up and
began to walk home across the fields beside the wheat.
Never gave up anything. Never needed to. For as long
as anyone can remember. How they looked. How it
beat down. Second-to-last. Disappearing or coming
into view. The work of it. Like music for which notes
have been written but nothing yet played.

Tipped over and drained spout. Memory a fluid, not a
solid. Drainpipe and chimney flue. At night "in a safe
place." *I want my money back*. Rearranging expectations.
No one emerges from the field already tall with barley.
Is there ever anyone in the yellow field at night. A
most-loved object. Slashes away at our cow hearts.
Makes its way here and stays. Seeps into my joints
until they bulge with it.

And the mother. The wall in front of me. "Come
out, come out, whoever you are hiding in the field
next to the house." And before it comes again, is it
a garden? Nobody wants to hear any more. We would.
"Show yourself." Because I am too fast/I am slow.
Tragedy is small, too. That we may appreciate our
fear. Can't be healed. *The arc of a Lover's conjecture.*

Yes, I want to have a way to separate these countries: each swallows the world that came before. *I am a continuing to, a daily continuing to.* She tried to paint it but the brush escapes. To recede and be noticed. Herself colorless. Up here closer to the window. Sometimes sliding down the left side. That wants to turn to red. What is that there behind you? Can't quite.

Each form becomes the next. Needle and eye. Listened all night to the faithful suffering of the dog. The man in the next cabin. Every afternoon. Hands full of the same things he left with. Imagining the hot skillet and the fillet flaking. I turned on my bed all night. Pre-mourning for a loss I anticipated. Everything else must encircle us: a precondition for the past.

Our bodies remember. Intricate trinkets beating out
the time. Bright bangles. Every line has its way of
cutting. I am just looking. They have come out
brown and round. Or just looking. We wipe away
the sticks. Rattling on the stones. Lined up
and separated. Angel to Jacob: from their kin. See
how graceful we are, dancing. [touches hip. dislocates.]

What happens when your name is changed. The dog
whining at my feet. For each incandesced along the
twinge. Why shouldn't we stand under the raining
quercus oaks. Stripping outside. *I will not let thee go except
thou bless me*. I want to set her on her feet. Twist me.
The frame glazed refracting while we are stepping
outside. Even then, until. To render luminous by heat.

They see differently. First it sounds like planes
coming up from the south. What good is a dark day
without rain? Throw me around, roll me on your
tongue. Transduction of light. Are you willing to
use the curved blade of a question. Who is ready?
I am ready and I am ready but *I* am not ready.

Entry is made possible when. Hide the ordinary.
They are designed to adhere. To take the sunlight
and equally the stone. Like a girl. We have scaled
each other. Tossing and following, turning and
riding off. The same look. One and other. I owe
you, you remember my debt. Carry me heavy.
No demarcation.

We may conclude it is not love. Everywhere we look. The past purges its aches. The need for the literal, for restoration a path back black ash. The golden cherries of that June the birds at the trees stripping the pits of flesh leaving them. What was it I was thinking last night when the rush came and I could hear you stirring deep beneath me. Strung along the branches. As if it were not mine. Not permanent.

That in the dark valleys began. But now I have.
Everywhere for winter but the other birds. Find
them disproportionate. November, its *nova, nova,* its
free fall the little flocks. Everything is smaller and
swifter than this. Time lets it be. In the tops of
cottonwoods. Few are faithless. In another country.
Bisected. You couldn't give a pear for my faithfulness.

Notes

page 21. The phrase "the loneliest sound I ever heard" was spoken in reference to Helen Keller's voice by a friend of hers.

page 33. Title from a line by Denise Levertov.

page 39. *lave*: in archaeology, the remains; what is left over.

page 53. *tondo*: circular painting or relief carving.

About the author

Kathleen Jesme is the author of two previous collections of poetry, *Motherhouse*, winner of the Lena-Miles Wever Todd Poetry Prize, and *Fire Eater*. She lives in Minnesota.

Ahsahta Press

Sawtooth Poetry Prize Series

2002: Aaron McCollough, *Welkin* (Brenda Hillman, judge)

2003: Graham Foust, *Leave the Room to Itself* (Joe Wenderoth, judge)

2004: Noah Eli Gordon, *The Area of Sound Called the Subtone* (Claudia Rankine, judge)

2005: Karla Kelsey, *Knowledge, Forms, The Aviary* (Carolyn Forché, judge)

2006: Paige Ackerson-Kiely, *In No One's Land* (D. A. Powell, judge)

2007: Rusty Morrison, *the true keeps calm biding its story* (Peter Gizzi, judge)

2008: Barbara Maloutas, *the whole Marie* (C. D. Wright, judge)

New Series

1. Lance Phillips, *Corpus Socius*
2. Heather Sellers, *Drinking Girls and Their Dresses*
3. Lisa Fishman, *Dear, Read*
4. Peggy Hamilton, *Forbidden City*
5. Dan Beachy-Quick, *Spell*
6. Liz Waldner, *Saving the Appearances*
7. Charles O. Hartman, *Island*
8. Lance Phillips, *Cur aliquid vidi*
9. Sandra Miller, *oriflamme.*
10. Brigitte Byrd, *Fence Above the Sea*
11. Ethan Paquin, *The Violence*
12. Ed Allen, *67 Mixed Messages*
13. Brian Henry, *Quarantine*
14. Kate Greenstreet, *case sensitive*
15. Aaron McCollough, *Little Ease*
16. Susan Tichy, *Bone Pagoda*
17. Susan Briante, *Pioneers in the Study of Motion*
18. Lisa Fishman, *The Happiness Experiment*
19. Heidi Lynn Staples, *Dog Girl*
20. David Mutschlecner, *Sign*
21. Kristi Maxwell, *Realm Sixty-four*
22. G. E. Patterson, *To and From*
23. Chris Vitiello, *Irresponsibility*
24. Stephanie Strickland, *Zone : Zero*
25. Charles O. Hartman, *New and Selected Poems*
26. Kathleen Jesme, *The Plum-Stone Game*

Ahsahta Press

MODERN AND CONTEMPORARY POETRY OF THE AMERICAN WEST

This book is set in Apollo MT type with Goudy Oldstyle titles
by Ahsahta Press at Boise State University
and manufactured according to the Green Press Initiative
by Thomson-Shore, Inc.
Cover design by Quemadura.
Book design by Janet Holmes.

AHSAHTA PRESS

2009

JANET HOLMES, DIRECTOR
BREONNA KRAFFT
AMBER NELSON
DAVID SCOTT
NAOMI TARLE
ROSS HARGREAVES, INTERN